"J. R. Solonche can pack so much humor and linguistic playfulness into such tight bundles, it feels like 1,000 clowns issuing from a VW Bug. He can also fit a lot of darkness and mortality into them, which feels more like 1,000 clowns dressed like Marilyn Manson issuing from a VW Bug. Solonche can be crass the way only the truthful can be, mischievous as a child with his hands in the honey jar, or even aphoristic and proverbial like a modern day Martial. Though you never know which Solonche you're going to encounter on the next page, he's a great bunch of guys to get to know."

— STEPHEN CRAMER is winner of the Louise Bogan Award and the National Poetry Series.

"The poems of J. R. Solonche catch the reader off guard in playful profundity. While always mindful of the tradition of poetry masquerading as direct statement (the like of W. C. Williams, Robert Bly, Robert Creeley, and Charles Bukowski), J. R. Solonche nevertheless 'makes it new' through his masterful use of understatement, aphorism, word play, and anaphora—raising poem after thoughtful poem from the familiar and often overlooked 'little things' of the poet's day-to-day encounter with the world."

— PHILLIP STERLING is author most recently of *And Then Snow*.

"Sample one by one these epigrammatic, epiphenomenal, Epicurean episodes as if they were puffs from a tower of pastry. Savor the zest of lemon, the pinch of sea salt, the dollop of crème fraiche, and the absence of any more sugar than necessary to ease the ingestion of truth. A feast for fanatics of language and lovers of pith. I'm not sure what pith is, but I know it when I see it."

—SARAH WHITE is author most recently of *Iridescent Guest.*

"Solonche, an accomplished poet, employs various forms in this compilation, including haiku, prose poem, and free verse. The poems often imaginatively enter into the natural or material world via anthropomorphic similes . . . Many works have an aphoristic quality that recall Zen koans, and they can be playfully amusing or even silly . . . A strong set of sympathetic but never sentimental observations."

—KIRKUS REVIEWS

"These short poems are an extraordinary amalgam of wit, close observation, humor, and clear-seeing. Each one singles out and illuminates an ordinary moment—ordinary, that is, until the poet explodes into a miniature epiphany. Easy of access and frequently profound, J. R. Solonche's poems induce in me a state of delighted surprise."

—CHASE TWICHELL is author of *Horses Where the Answers Should Have Been: New and Selected Poems.*

"In a style that favors brevity and pith, J. R. Solonche brings a richness of experience, observation, and wit into his poems. Here is the world! they exclaim. And here and here and here! Watched over by ancient lyric gods—Time, Death, and Desire—we find the quotidian here transformed."

—CHRISTOPHER NELSON is editor of *Green Linden Press*.

"The history of book blurbs is littered with high falutin' praise, whacky and wild metaphors, written to impress not to inform. All I need to say about J. R. Solonche's poems is that they are good, really, really good. So much so that they have a high 'I-wish-I'd-written-that' factor. That's a compliment I hand out to very few poets writing today. You want wit? You want humor? You want erudition? You want them all mixed into poems? Try Solonche. You won't be disappointed. Envious perhaps, but not disappointed."

—JOHN MURPHY is editor of *The Lake Contemporary Poetry Webzine*.

"The best feature of Solonche's poetry is its diversity. Everyone who encounters this volume (including the postman who delivers it to you) will find something in it to understand and remember—and a great deal to enjoy."

—TONY BEYER is author of *Anchor Stone*, finalist for the New Zealand Book Award.

THE EGLANTINE

J. R. SOLONCHE

SHANTI ARTS PUBLISHING

BRUNSWICK, MAINE

Published by Shanti Arts Publishing

Designed by Shanti Arts Designs

Source of image on cover and page 4 is Rawpexel.com/stock.adobe.com; source of image on pp. 16–17 and 56–57 is OlgaShashok/stock.adobe.com.

Shanti Arts LLC

193 Hillside Road

Brunswick, Maine 04011

shantiarts.com

Printed in the United States of America

ISBN: 978-1-962082-00-6

Library of Congress Control Number: 2023943108

TITLES BY THIS AUTHOR

CONTENTS

ACKNOWLEDGMENTS

The American Journal of Poetry: "1965"
Fugue: "Fairy Table"
The Lake: "Utilities"
Poetry Northwest: "The Eglantine"
Verse-Virtual: "The Influence of Fifteen Anxieties"

Part I

ECHOES

With the hummingbirds
gone, the yellowjackets
have the feeder to themselves,
and when they are gone, the air
will be a little sweeter there.

TOAD

Look, there's a frog, my daughter said pointing to a toad
in the grass. Oh, that's not a frog. That's a toad, I said. But
it looks like a frog. It just has bumps all over it, she said.
That's right. They're related. You could say they're cousins,
I said. But toads are ugly. Frogs are much handsomer, she
said. True. But when you kiss a toad in a fairy tale, it turns
into a handsome prince, I said. Not a handsome frog? she
said. No, a handsome prince, I said. Not an ugly prince?
she said. No, a handsome prince, I said. That's stupid. That
doesn't make any sense, she said. Well, it's a fairy tale, I said.
What's a fairy tale anyway? Is it a story about fairies? she
said. Actually, most of them aren't stories about fairies. I
guess they are stories that fairies tell, I said. Stories fairies
tell to us? she said. More like stories fairies tell one another,
I said. Well, fairy tales are stupid. When I grow

up I'm going to write a fairy tale that makes sense, she said. You don't have to wait until you grow up. You can write one now, I said. And so she did. And here it is: *Once upon a time, there was an ugly toad with bumps all over who wanted to be a handsome frog who was smooth all over, so he wished upon a star with all his might, and while he slept, the moon came down from the sky and kissed him, and when he woke up, he was a handsome frog who was smooth all over. The End.* That's very good, but did he live happily ever after? You can't write *The End* until you say he lived happily ever after, I said. Well, he didn't live happily ever after, she said. Why not? I said. Because he was still alone. He was happy to be alone when he was a toad, but he wasn't happy anymore when he became a frog, she said. I see. You were right. That is a fairy tale that makes sense, I said.

WHAT IF PROMETHEUS

What if Prometheus
hadn't gone and done it,
hadn't stolen the gods' fire,
hadn't given it to us?
Where would we be?
What would we be doing now
in the dark, in the cold, in our ignorance?
All our ages would be our dark ages.
All our meals would be raw meat,
raw roots that break our teeth.
We'd all be all thumbs.
We'd all be high school dropouts.
We'd all be bums.

ALL RIGHT

I came upon a dead squirrel on the road.
There was no blood.
That was unusual.
There is usually blood.
But it was dead all right.
There was no doubt about that.
"I'm all right with it," it said.
"It was quick. It was painless.
I didn't see it coming," it said.
"I got hit just right. I didn't bleed at all," it said.
"My brother was hit yesterday.
He bled profusely from the head.
He was a mess.
But I'm all right with it," it said.
I nodded and went on walking.

MY SHADOW

After all these many years
of following me around and
leading me by the nose and for
just a minute without movement
disappearing under my skin,
today my shadow finally
introduced himself to me.
However, under threat of death,
I cannot speak his name.

AFTER A MORNING

After a morning of overcast,
the sun cast itself over
the clouds long enough
to light up noon,
then went undercover
again to spy on the afternoon.

SHORT CONVERSATION WITH THE SUN

"Where are you going?"
I asked the sun which was
going away. "I am going
down behind the trees
across the road and then
behind the horizon beyond
the trees and then behind
the earth beyond the horizon,"
the sun said. "Why do you ask?"
"I always ask my friends
where they are going when
they leave me," I said.

AFTER THE EARLY

After the early
fall frost of overnight,
the marigolds lost
some, but some more
still held their own
still holding their own.

TRUTH

I asked my mathematician friend
if mathematics is an invention
or a discovery, for I had been
wondering about it a long time.
It's both, he said. First it was a
discovery and then it was an
invention. I thought so, I said.
It's just like poetry, which first
was a discovery and then was
an invention, except that poetry
keeps reinventing itself while
mathematics doesn't. It's done.
That's because mathematics has
already discovered the truth, so it
doesn't need to keep reinventing

itself as poetry does, he said.
The trouble is that you poets keep
looking for the truth in the wrong
places. Oh, where's that? I said.
In your hearts, he said. You'll
never find the truth there. You'll
only keep finding the same old lies.
Maybe so, I said. But you have to
admit that you guys need us. For
what? We already have our one
beautiful truth, he said. Yes, I said.
But you need us and our thousands
of beautiful lies to let you bear your
one and only beautiful truth.

HYDRANGEA

I have never seen a flower
look as happy as the hydrangea
here in the deer fence on the other
side of the deer. In a year or two,
it will take it over. And that will be
as all right with me as anything
has ever been all right with me.
There's not much worse than
having to look at unhappy flowers.

RED

Now that the hummingbirds
have left, I'm thinking of leaving
the empty feeder out all fall
and all winter. I'm not sure why.
It's a whim. You don't need to
be sure of a whim, but maybe
it's because I want to see what
it looks like covered in snow.
I bet it looks like a red rose
covered in snow or a cardinal
covered in snow or the red hot
center of summer covered in snow.

CARMEN

If the *tamias striatus*
scurrying around
out here gathering
all the *medulla panis*
I threw on the ground
weren't called *chipmunks*,
I'd write a *carmen* about them.

THE GOLDEN QUESTION

Have you ever waited
for someone to ask you
the question for which
you had, years before,
already prepared
the answer? You know
the question I mean.
The question that never came.
The question that never does.
The Golden Question.

ON MY AFTERNOON WALK

On my afternoon walk
I found a book. I've found
newspapers. I've found
porno magazines. I've
found banks statements.
I've found electric bills.
I've found notebooks
thrown out of cars by high
school seniors after their
last class in June. This was
the first time I found a book.
It was a hardcover novel,
The Policewomen's Bureau.
It was signed by the author,
Edward Conlon, a "New York

Times Bestselling Author."
I was curious. I read the first
sentence while walking home.
"Policewoman Marie Carrara
had a feeling something
meaningful had happened,
but she'd be damned if she
knew what it was." Not bad,
I thought. A pretty good hook.
But if I were Conlon's editor,
I would have changed it to
"Call me Marie Carrara,
Policewoman." So much
better, don't you think?

THE LEAST I CAN DO

I'm doing for him what I do for nearly no one.
I'm reading his book.
I'm reading his book from beginning to end.
I'm reading every blessed word.
It's the least I can do for him who inscribed it,
"With gratitude and admiration."

TODAY THE SKY WAS TWO SKIES

Today the sky was two skies.
There was the blue sky with white clouds.
There was the overcast, gray sky right next to it.
It was a civil war of sorts of skies.
The thunder from the south was the first shot fired.

I HATE "I CAN'T COMPLAIN"

"How are you?" I ask a neighbor.
"Oh, I can't complain," he says.
I hate when he says that.
It's not true.
I've heard him complain to Pete the postmaster
in the post office.
"How are you?" I ask another neighbor.
"Oh, I can't complain," she says.
I hate when she says that.
It's not true.
I've heard her complain to the librarian in the library.
I know it's simply a greeting.

I know we are not supposed to take it seriously.
I know we're supposed to smile and go on our way.
But sometimes I wish they would complain.
I'm a good listener.
I'll listen to their marriage woes.
I'll listen to their health problems.
I'll listen to them carry on about their grown children.
I'll listen to them gripe about taxes.
I was a psychology major before I switched to English.
Besides it will give me an excuse to complain to them.
I'm tired of listening to me complain to no one but myself .

THE FOOL

The fool is the wisest among them.
The fool is the most cowardly among them.
The fool is the bravest among them.
The fool is the smallest among them.
The fool is the profanest among them.
The fool is the purest among them.
The fool is the most honest among them.
The fool is the loneliest among them.
The fool is the bravest among them.
The fool is the saddest among them.
The fool has the best lines among them.

OCTOBER

The yellow marigolds
and the orange marigolds
feel the chill happen around them.
The yellow marigolds
feel the yellow leaves fall upon them.
The orange marigolds
feel the orange leaves fall upon them.
Nevertheless, they still feel for the sun.
Nevertheless, the sun still feels for them
and shines on shining on them.

ILLEGIBLE

The poem I wrote last night is illegible.
I scribbled it hastily in the dark without my glasses.
I was hoping I could read it anyway this morning.
But it is still illegible.
One word only is legible.
The word is *mind*.
But, in truth, it could be *wind*.
So what?
They're the same, aren't they?

MARRIAGE

"Marriage is a prison," she said.
She was my friend's second wife.
"But you've been married for only two years," I said.
"That's long enough to know," she said.
She ought to know.
This was her third marriage.
Not all prison cells are the same, I suppose.

CHICKENS

My neighbor keeps chickens.
I hear their obnoxious voices.
Thank heaven I am not a rooster,
for then I would have to copulate
with these filthy things.

ENOBARBUS

Did you know that I
am the only character
in all of Shakespeare
who dies of a broken
heart? Well, maybe
Ophelia does in a way
before she drowns.
And it's possible that
Desdemona could have
if she had had the time.
And Othello, too. But
Shakespeare put them
out of their misery.
Not me. Nope, not me.

BARKING

My neighbor's dog is barking.
It is a loud, deep, confident bark.
It is the bark of an animal that knows who it is.
I wish I could bark like that.
I would bark at everyone and everything.
I would be the best damn barker in the neighborhood.
I would bark up every tree, right or wrong.
My bark would be my bite.

GOD

"God has a brown voice, as soft and full as beer."
—Anne Sexton

God has blue eyes, as icy and empty as the sky.

God has red hair and a red beard, as fierce as the fires of hell.

God has callused hands, as hard as dragon skin.

God has false teeth, as false as all the false messiahs.

God has a big nose, as hooked as the Jew.

God has the odor of sanctity, as foul as the odor of sanctity.

TWO TURTLES IN OCTOBER

What are they doing here,
on that log
in the swamp water
in October?
Poor turtles.
They are just as confused
as we are,
and they won't protect us either,
our shells.

EVEN THE WHISTLE OF THE TRAIN
IS NOT THE SAME

In the ear of October,
even the whistle of the train is not the same.
It is red when it was green.
It is orange when it was green.
It is brown when it was green.
It is yellow when it was green.
It falls from the locomotive of the train.
It covers the tracks.
It falls into the ears.
It smothers them.

OCTOBER IS NOT SOBER

It's the drunkard of the year.
It sees pink elephants in the orange oaks.
It stumbles along the red road.
It falls on its face.
It falls again.
It falls some more.
It slurs its speech.
Its speech is colorful even slurred.
It is intoxicated on dying marigolds, yellower than ever.

OCTOBER DOES NOT LAST LONG ENOUGH

It should be the longest of the year.
It has the most to offer.
It has the most color.
September should move over.
November should move over.
They should let October elbow them aside.
September and November should defer to October.
September should give ten days to October.
November should give ten days to October.

HARVEST OF HEARTS

There is no known season for harvesting hearts.
Every season is open season on hearts.
They are ripe for harvesting regardless of the month.
They begin in the breast but migrate
to ripen in the mouth.
That's when you know your heart is in your mouth.
It tastes ripe in your mouth.
But not for poets.
Poets are different from us.
That's when poets know their mouth is in their heart.
Thank goodness for poets.
Poets are always different from us.
That is why we need poets.
Not because we need poetry.
Because they are different from us.

SPHINX

Do you think that's all the Sphinx said?
What else do you think the Sphinx said?
Do you think she said, "Whose head do you have?"
Do you think she said, "Whose body do you have?"
Do you think she said, "You look like a sand flea?"
Do you think she said, "Yet you made me?"
Do you think she said, "I felt your hammer and your chisel?"
Do you think she said, "Do not think, however,
that I am your slave?"
Do you think she said, "You are my slaves,
you who made me?"
Do you think she said, "My greatest gift is my silence?"
Do you think she said, "Be thankful?"
Do you think this is a riddle?
Do you think she said, "Be thankful?"
Do you think your guess is as good as mine?

ON THE WALL OF THE HOSPITAL ROOM

On the wall of my hospital room,
above the mirror above the sink,
there is a wooden crucifix
with the figure of Christ in pewter.
His arms are stretched outward
and upward and forward slightly
in benediction or as though ready
to execute a swan dive, preparing
himself mentally, finding his
balance on the balls of his feet,
and he is wearing a strange robe
that seems to give to his back
a closed set of wings, like the carapace
that beetles have over their real wings.

MORNING CONVERSATION

This morning I found
the smallest flowers
I have ever seen. "Why
you're the smallest
flowers I've ever seen,"
I said to the tiny flowers
growing in the narrow
crack between the paving
stones. "Yes, we know
how small we are," they
said. "But, look, you did
notice us, didn't you?"
"Yes, but only because
you are alone down there
in that crack. There's no
one else to notice," I said.
"We grow where we can.
It's our sun, too, you know,"
they said. "Of all people,
a poet ought to know that
we must grow where we can,
in the narrowest narrow
cracks of the world."

Part II

THE INFLUENCE OF FIFTEEN ANXIETIES

—with apologies to Harold Bloom

1

I cut myself shaving this morning. It took a
long time for the bleeding to stop.
I know it's foolish, but for a moment, I
thought I was going to bleed to death.

2

Every time I approach that intersection with
the four stop signs, I get anxious.
I know what to do. I worry that the other
two or three drivers won't, though.

3

I usually don't have a problem flying, but the last
time I flew to San Francisco I had an anxiety
attack. That's why I asked my doctor
for a prescription for Ativan.

4
Last summer, a big tree next to the house came
down during a severe thunder storm. It missed
the house, but I still had two other
trees cut down just in case.

5
I like to sit outside to write. I like to drink a
bourbon cocktail while I write. However,
yellow jackets also like bourbon cocktails. I've
been stung more than once over the years, so
they make me a little nervous.

6
A pair of barred owls have been nesting in the
woods behind the house. Often I hear them
calling to each other. I get very anxious
when one fails to answer.

7
My daughter is a good driver. She's never had
an accident. Nevertheless, I worry when
she goes to work. Especially if it's raining or
foggy. I tell her to take the Subaru Crosstrek.
It has all-wheel drive and fog lights. I worry even
more if she has to use that old Hyundai.

8
Going to the dentist used to make me anxious. It doesn't
anymore. I refuse the needle. The way I see it, a few
minutes of pain is preferable to a few hours of numbness.
And the pretty dental assistant thinks I'm really tough.

9
Although the economy is good and my portfolio is doing well,
I'm still anxious about the markets. The experts on the radio
predict a recession in the second or third quarter of 2020.

10
Power cutting tools make me nervous. When I go to
a hardware store and see the circular saws and the
chain saws, I sweat and my hands start to tremble.

11

When I was a kid, and even a teenager, getting a
shot was an ordeal. I was so anxious, I fainted. I
fainted from polio shots. I fainted from measles
shots. I fainted from flu shots. I fainted from
penicillin shots. My mother must have been disappointed.
She knew then and there I'd never be a doctor.

12

Motorcycles scare me to death. I rode one once. I fell off. I
wasn't hurt because I was going about 15 miles per hour and
fell on grass. Nevertheless, I'll never get on one again. Not
as long as I live. Like I said, those things scare me to death.

13

I used to enjoy bicycle riding. So much so that I purchased
a $1200 state-of-the-art bike with a carbon fiber frame, disc
brakes, and 20 speeds. It was great. I loved it. However,
I was very apprehensive about riding it on the roads
around here. A lot of people drove too fast. I was very
nearly side-swiped a couple of times. I was so
nervous about it, I donated it to charity.

14

I like hiking. We used to take hikes that lasted
days. For example, on the Long Trail in Vermont.
The woods of the northeast are black bear
habitat. Because I was afraid of encountering
a black bear, especially a mother with cubs, I would sing
as I walked. My favorite song was "Always Look on the
Bright Side of Life" from Monty Python's *Life of Brian*.

15

For several years, I sang with a chorus. It wasn't
professional, but they were good. Many members were
trained singers and could sing on pitch, even when the
conductor mixed up the sections during rehearsals. I
was fine as long as I could hide in the middle of the
bass section, but I was very apprehensive when it came
to solos. I did manage to get through them but only
with the help of bourbon just before the concert. If
the altos smelled it on my breath, they never said.

DEATH HAS BEEN HERE

Death has been here.
You can tell.
You can smell the tell-tale smell.
You can see his handiwork.
You can see his signature
in the lower right hand corner.
Somewhere close is the body death left behind.
It is right here under your nose.
Only the dead remains remain.
Only the dead to attest that death has been here,
but when he's in a good mood,
and he displays the hollow stalks splayed yellow,
death is even beautiful in his way.

THE SCARECROWS

It's not hard to scare them up
if you want to see them,
the scarecrows, plentiful in the yards,
on the lawns and the porches,
but one in the cornfields?
The real ones I mean in the real cornfields?
No, they haven't been there for years.
And that's because they haven't been here for years.

SAD SIMILE

A day
without
a poem
is like
nothing else
I know.

MY NEIGHBOR

My neighbor
is playing
with her dog.
She is making
strange sounds
I cannot spell.

PRIZE OR PROPOSITION

Let me put it
this way:

If either one
turned up,

I wouldn't
turn it down.

GRAY

The old birdhouse
is so old it has turned
the gray of the ash tree
it's hanging on.

SONNET

Where were you when you last saw it?
Were you inside or outside?
Which side were you on, the north side or the south side?
Where was the sun?
Was the sun over left shoulder or your right shoulder?
What were you doing when you saw it last?
Were you talking on the telephone?
Were you walking up the stairs?
Were you driving on the highway?
Were you driving on the back roads?
Were you daydreaming?
Were you distracted?
Were you remembering that kiss?
Were you watching it watching you?

1965

It was 1965.
I dropped out of college.
I was 1-A.
So the letter came.
It was a greeting card from Uncle Sam.
"Greetings," it said.
So I went to Whitehall Street.
It was 5 AM.
It was dark.
It was drizzling.
It was dreary.
I was scared shit.
But I had the letter from Dr. Bearman.
It said I had albuminuria.
I don't know why Dr. Bearman thought that would get me out.
But it was all I had.
I recognized a few from high school.

Goldstein was there.
Weintraub was there.
Grazzioli was there.
But he wasn't drafted.
He was there to join the Marines.
I had a clipboard.
I went from line to line.
I went from station to station.
I passed everything.
But I had my letter which I hadn't shown yet.
I didn't know which doctor to show it to.
Wasn't there a kidney doctor to show it to?
I was running out of doctors.
The last station was the eye exam.
"Take off your glasses and read the last line
on the chart," the sergeant said.
I knew he was a sergeant.
I had seen sergeants in movies.
I recognized the stripes.
I took off my glasses.
I couldn't see the last line.

I couldn't see the chart.

I could barely see the wall.

"I can't read it," I said.

"Give me those glasses," the sergeant said.

I gave him my glasses.

He put them under some kind of microscope.

He shook his head.

He wrote "Z" next to my right eye.

He wrote "Z" next to my left eye.

"What does "Z" mean?" I asked.

"It means you're Zeed out," he said.

He gave me my clipboard.

"You're 4-F. You're fucking blind," he said.

"Thank you," I said.

So I didn't need Dr. Bearman's letter.

So I didn't need albuminuria.

So I didn't need a kidney doctor.

So I just needed my eyes.

So I thanked my father for his Z eyes.

So I thanked my grandfather for his Z eyes.

So I thanked my great-grandfather for his Z eyes.

So I thanked my lucky Z stars.

I WANT TO KNOW WHY THERE IS
SO MUCH TO CARE ABOUT

I want to know why there is so much to care about.
I want to know why there is not enough music in the world
to take care of it.
I want to know why there is only so much and no more.
I want to know why there is too much to bear.
I want to know why the suffering will last longer than all the
music in the world.
I want to know why the grief will outlive all the music for
the dead.
I want to know when it's time for the music to sing the
words to sleep.
I want to know when it's time for the music to sing itself to sleep.

I want to know when it's time to sing the songs of silver.
I want to know when it's time to wear the shirt of thorns.
I want to know when it's time to wear the robe of ashes.
I want to know when it's time to play the horn of horn.
I want to know when it's time to walk in the sandals of sand.
I want to know when it's time to wield the thigh bone high
above me.
I want to know when it's time for words to fail us.
I want to know why our words are lead and thereby useless.
I want to know why our words are born dead.
I want to know how to make the smallest coffins for the
smallest bodies.
I want to know what prayer is the prayer to say at the burial.
I want to know what silence will last as the last silence for all
their eternities.

LEAVES

A strong gust of wind
has shot so many yellow
leaves off the trees
in one shot,
I thought the sun
had shorted out and shattered
itself against the sharp cloud-rocks.

TWENTY-FIVE POEMS BEGINNING
WITH LINES BY EMILY DICKINSON

1
My wheel is in the dark.
It turns and turns and turns
but never leaves its mark.
Only the friction burns.

2
Impossibility like wine
improves with years.
Impossibility is just fine
with all my possible fears.

3
It was a quiet way
that I took, the dead-
end one from town today.
The only noise was in my head.

4

In winter in my room
is just like in summer in my room
is just like in autumn in my room
is just like springtime in my room.

5

Doom is the house without the door,
but it does have windows all around
and walls and a polished floor
and property on which its bound.

6

I took my power in my hand.
I stroked it down and up,
stood it straight and let it stand
until it filled up half a cup.

7

I had no cause to be awake.
My dream was all my wakefulness,
containing everything for the sake
of waking life as is blessed to bless.

8

I'd rather recollect a setting
than set a recollection.
I'd rather direct the getting
than get the wrong direction.

9

Down time's quaint stream
I row, row, row my boat,
but life's not but a dream.
Can't swim? Learn at least to float.

10

It is a lonesome glee,
the joke I share with only me.
It is the echo of a laugh,
the one I do on your behalf.

11

Delight is as the flight.
Leave it there, right there.
Do not say of what it might.
Just leave delight hanging in air.

12

I am alive I guess.
A guess as good as it gets.
As good as the guess of Descartes.
Even though I'm not as smart.

13

To my small hearth his fire came.
You can't fool me, Miss Emily.
All your excuses are lame.
I know what this is all about – precisely.

14

If I could tell how glad I was,
I wouldn't tell how glad.
I wouldn't tell because
I want to seem, just seem, a little mad.

15

When continents expire,
the earth still goes its way.
Even when the oceans catch fire,
the galaxy has nothing at all to say.

16

Take all away,
all that is meaningless.
I'll tell you what must stay
when down to one or less.

17

Finding is the first act.
Finding out the second.
Finding out the fact
the third. And last, I reckon.

18

Four trees upon a solitary acre
sounds like you've studied Zen.
Of course, this is pure conjecture,
but what else could it mean then?

19

If I should die
before I've finished this,
do it for me (Sigh),
or just give it a kiss.

20
Of silken speech and specious shoe
I have no more to say.
So give alliteration all its due.
Stand back, and let the esses have their way.

21
Those not live yet
cannot hear this.
If they could, they would forget
what was their bliss.

22
This is a blossom of the brain.
Whether a daisy or a rose,
whether sense or insane,
it's what that organ chose.

23

The admirations and contempts of time
are all that matter.
Every other is merest mime
or childish chatter.

24

Remembrance has a rear and front
but not apparently a silhouette.
Always it's the back to me or the brunt
burnt into what I can't forget.

25

What is "Paradise" you asked.
You did not ask it, "Paradise is where?"
Therefore you. like me, are tasked
to find it nowhere else but here.

HOW BRAVELY

How bravely
the marigolds
wear the wet
snow come so
eerily early late
in October,
but see how,
nevertheless,
they are the
worse for wear.

NOTE TO SARAH

I watched the Zoom
reading you sent me,
Sarah, but please
don't tell me that this
is the future of poetry.
I liked yours well enough
and another one or two,
but poetry has to take place
in one room, you know,
the way school used to be
a long, long time ago.

THE ONLY SPOT

The only spot
with sun
this afternoon
was out back
by the old stump
of the ash tree
I had cut down
twenty years ago,
so I set my chair
there, put
my feet up on
the stump,
closed my eyes,
and dreamed
the whole ash
tree back again.

AT LEAST THAT WAS TRUE

Should everything be true?
I said to Jim.
Jim teaches philosophy.
What do you mean? Jim said.
I mean must everything be true?
Why can't some things, or even one thing, be false?
Why should anything be false? he said.
For the fun of it, I said. For the poetry of it.
Such as? he said.
Such as, The moon is made of green cheese.
That's not true, I said, but it is fun.
And it's poetry.
It is fun to believe in one false thing.
Perhaps. But what's more important?
Fun or the truth? he said.
Poetry is the most important, I said.
And poetry doesn't have to be true, but the truth does.
The truth can be fun, too.
Sometimes it's more fun than poetry, he said.
I had to admit.
It was true.

I'VE ALWAYS WANTED TO BE AN AUTHORITY

I've always wanted to be an authority.
An authority on anything.
An authority on the one-room school house.
An authority on the native tribes of New Jersey.
An authority on the Rolls-Royce automobile.
An authority on the Dead Sea.
An authority on the Viking longship.
An authority on hummingbirds.
An authority on the printing press.
An authority on Chinese poetry.
An authority on Jewish gangsters.
An authority on beer.
I've always wanted to be the authority the world looked to.
The authority on anything.
The authority on wanting to be an authority.

THE WIND GUSTS

The wind gusts
were so strong,
they stripped
the birch tree
bare in minutes,
then tried to rip
the twigs away,
but between
the gusts I heard
the birch tree
order them to stay.

ONE FROM EACH

One from each
I take refreshment.

One from each
as if it were a spring.

One from each
comes forth from under.

One from each
beneath my chair here.

One from each
is all they can afford.

One from each
is tithe of their affection.

One from each
is tribute of the tribe.

HE WAS THE TALK OF THE TOWN

He was the talk of the town.
He was the town talker.
He talked to himself.
He talked a blue streak.
He talked a mean streak.
He talked in his sleep.
To him talk was cheap.
In the bar, he talked it up.
In the flea market, he talked it down.
He talked circles around the words.
He talked the words into it.

INDIAN SUMMER

Autumn is on hold.
The fall falls for it.
The trees take a breath and count to ten.
The leaves regroup for a better grip.
The wind warms its hands.
The turtles rise to the occasion from the mud.
They sunbathe on the log of summer again.
The redheaded woodpecker nosedives into
the ash tree as usual.
Its message is the same.
And the bees come out of hiding to no flowers.

THE SUN TURNS SILVER

The sun turns silver.
It wants to be the moon.
It is tired of gold.
It wants to see in the dark.
It has two inches of sky left to it.
But it does not want its reputation tarnished.
So I said, "Could you be the moon for my sake?
I will tell no one, and I will never ask again."
"Yes," the sun said. "I will be the moon for your sake
as long you tell no one and never ask again."
So the sun was the moon for my sake,
and I have told no one and have never asked again.

PARLORS

Some have parlors in their houses.
I have never had a parlor.
Would I have been paler if I had had a parlor?
I wish I had a parlor.
There is something grand about a parlor.
There is something gold about a parlor.
There is something silver about a parlor.
There is something convex about a parlor.
There is something velvet about a parlor.
A parlor is erotic.
A parlor is romantic.
A parlor reminds me of umbrellas.
A parlor reminds me of kid gloves.
A parlor reminds me of removing kid gloves finger by finger.
A parlor reminds me of flowers here and flowers here
and flowers here.
A parlor reminds me of Chopin.
A parlor reminds me of tricks.
A parlor reminds me of games.
A parlor reminds me of notes on
small cards in small envelopes.
A parlor reminds me of a gentleman.
A parlor reminds me of a lady.
A parlor reminds me of one kid glove left behind
intentionally on the table
by the lady in the parlor.

MY CHAIR

I have placed my chair between
the woods and the feeder, in
the middle of the flight path
of the birds. I want the chickadees
and titmice, the cardinals and
nuthatches to fly above me, to fly
to my right and to my left, to whiz
within inches of my head. I want
to hear the beating of their wings as
they speed by. I want to close my
eyes. I want to feel the sun warm
on my face and on my eyes. I want
to feel the sun warm on their wings
and on the sound of their wings and
on the soft strength of the breathing
of their wings. I want to imagine
what the next world, the world that
I know does not exist, must sound like.

SWANS IN THE MONTH OF NOVEMBER

Swans have long white necks in the month of November.
Swans have wide white wings in the month of November.
Swans undulate on the water in the month of November.
Swans are as swans always are in the month of November.
Swans, I hope you know what you are doing in the month of November.

CHILDREN'S BOOK

I want to write a children's book.
I want to write a book that children will read and remember.
I want to write a book that children will learn by heart.
I want to write a book that children will read to their children.
I want to write a book that they will recite by heart with their children.
I want to write a book with the rhymes book and look.
I want to write a book with the rhymes rhyme and time.
I want to write a book with the rhymes moon and loon.
I want to write a big book for little hands to hold.
I want to write a big book with big letters.
I want to write a book with words of one syllable only.
I want to write a book with the best little words in the best little order.
I want to write a book with a little to say.
I do not want to write a book with little to say.
I want to write a book even if it says so itself.

UTILITIES

I called the utility company.
I had an issue I needed taken care of.
Alex answered the phone.
He asked for my account number.
I told him I didn't know my account number.
I told him I throw away the bills after I pay them.
I told him I could give him any other information.
I gave him my phone number.
I gave him my street address.
I gave him my mailing address.
I gave him my Social Security number,
I gave him my mother's maiden name, Karp.
He laughed.
He had a sense of humor.
I like that.
He said he didn't need that.
He said at least it wasn't carp as in the fish.
I told him I once caught a carp.
I caught it in my lake.
It must have weighed 20 pounds.

I caught it on 8 pound test.

It was too heavy to get into the boat.

I asked him if he fished at all.

He said he did.

He said he preferred fly fishing.

He said he goes up to the Catskills to fish for trout.

I told him I tried fly casting once.

I couldn't do it.

I asked him if he likes beer.

He said he does.

I asked him if he had ever been to Trout Town Brewery.

It's in Roscoe, a famous trout fishing spot.

He said he was.

He said that's his favorite place for trout fishing followed by beer.

We spent the next 15 minutes talking about beer.

I said it was great talking to him.

He said it was great talking to me.

We hung up.

I realized I hadn't taken care of my issue.

I called the utility company again.

I took care of my issue with Melissa.

FAIRY TABLE

"Is the Sleeping Beauty a fairy table?"
—Emily, age 4½

No. However, it is the most important
piece of furniture in the fairy family's
house. It is where the fairy family dines,

and around it the whole fairy family's life
revolves. At the fairy table, father fairy
tells of his hard day at the office selling

fairy insurance, mother fairy tells of her day
at the hairdresser, the mall, the fitness center,
the soccer game, junior and sis fairy tell

of their day at school. At the fairy table,
the fairy family celebrates birthdays
and anniversaries. At the fairy table,

grandmother fairy prepares Christmas
dinner, aunt fairy prepares Thanksgiving
dinner, and uncle fairy carves the turkey

and the ham. At the fairy table, cousin fairy
throws mashed potatoes at junior fairy,
and sis fairy spills milk in her lap.

At the fairy table, mother fairy plays
bridge with her fairy friends, and father fairy
loses his shirt at poker every Friday night.

A DIALOGUE

One: I did not know what you knew.

Other: What I know I know because of you.

One: Suddenly it has grown cold.

Other: What should I remember about you?

One: Nothing has changed.

Other: Once you were larger than life. Now you are loose change in the pocket of my heart.

One: The future had your profile.

Other: I will save us.

One: I have already saved us.

BLACK IS NOT THE COLOR OF FEAR

Black is not the color of fear.
Gray is the color of fear.

I see it through the window in the sky.
It is the sky, end to end, back

to front, through and through,
oceans of gray with no center,

oceans of gray with no heart,
oceans of gray with no breath,

oceans of gray with no voice,
oceans of gray with no end in sight

like a long habit we cannot be done with,
which we are afraid for our lives to be done with.

KNOWLEDGE

The crimson azalea on
the threshold of bloom
doesn't know any more than
it needs to. The chickadee
in the crimson azalea doesn't
know any more than it needs to.
I, who watch the bird hop in
the bush, already know more
than I need to. Of course,
it can be argued that
I don't know what I need.

ON MY WALK BY THE MARSH

On my walk by the marsh,
I heard the cry
of a red-winged blackbird.
By the time I walked back,
I had learned it by heart.
Why not? It was the cry
of the only bird
in the marsh all that time.

THREE TRACTORS

Today I saw three tractors.
One was red.

One was green.
One was orange.

The only one I remember is the orange one.
Orange must be the best color for a tractor.

THE SKY TURNS TO ITS BUSINESS

The sky turns to its business
ignoring the dead leaves.
The trees turn in. They harden
to the cold winds coming.
So now to begin the end, for
it is beginning again as always.
As always I try to understand
your concern with the past.
I try hard, hard to be what a man
better than I would be now.
I try hard to understand why
you must reach back so often
to that place where you were all
together and completely happy. Was
it because you couldn't see over
the heads of father, of mother, of sister?
Was it because the beds were castle walls?

APOLOGY TO MY SOUL

Soul, I am sorry.
Soul, I apologize to you.
I extend a profound and hearty apology from the heart.
I did not believe you existed.
I did not believe that it was you spoke to me all this time.
How could I?
I never saw you.
You were invisible.
I could barely hear you over the noises of the world.
I could hardly hear you through the noises of the body.
You whisper.
I think you must suffer from laryngitis.
You do not show your face.
You do not show yourself.
I think you are afraid to show yourself.
Are you ugly?
Are you disfigured?
Are you a sideshow freak?
Never mind.
That is history.
That is all in the past.

I hear you now.
I recognize your voice.
I can tune out all the noises of the world.
I can turn down the noises of the body.
I can zero in on you, Soul.
So I am sorry that I doubted your existence.
I am sorry that I doubted you.
Do you forgive me, Soul?
Of course, you do.
Of course, you forgive me.
That is what you do.
That is what you are for.
That is what you are good for.
That is all you are good for.
Forgiveness is your forte.
It is your talent.
It is your genius.
Yes, Soul, you are the genius of forgiveness.
O, Soul.
O, fine, fine soul of mine.
I'm fine with you.

I WANTED TO MAKE A COVENANT WITH THE WIND

I wanted to make
a covenant with the wind,
so I went up
to the high space of the hill,

the meeting place
of the two roads,
and there
I promised the wind

that I would give
the wind
the voice and the motion
of my mind

if the wind promised
in exchange
to give me the motion
and the voice

of its no-mind
in the branches of the birch
and in the curly leaves
of the weeping willow,

but the wind
had no interest
in such a covenant
with me,

for the wind
had no use
for my mind's voice
and my mind's motion.

It moved in my hair
and moved in my sleeves
and moved in the grass
next to my feet

and moved
in the curly leaves
of the willow
behind me

and moved
in the branches
of the birch
behind the willow.

And then I went down
from the high space
of the hill with my covenant
in my hand.

POETRY

I walked into the used book store.
I asked the woman for Poetry.
She looked up and pointed behind her.
I went there, between Fiction and Biography,
and found four shelves of books.
I browsed among them for a while,
an old horse in a grassy meadow. One looked
interesting. It was The Vision of Sir Launfal
by James Russell Lowell.
It was a hundred years old.
The illustrations were beautiful.
The paper was silken and hardly yellowed.
But I didn't want to spend the twenty dollars for it.
My wife and daughter came in.
They were looking for me to show me the sunset.
We went out to watch it over the ocean.
It was beautiful.
It was a vision of the sun setting in the ocean.
It was a copper coin in a beggar's bowl.

THE EGLANTINE

The last word you hear as you leave the room is the word
you remember. It is the word that becomes your shadow
for an hour, that shares your shape, that you hear over
and over again, that becomes a bell to warn you of a place
without meaning. The last word you hear as you leave the
room entangles you in sweet briar. You did not notice
when the compromises began. Perhaps you have always
compromised. As soon as the dream found a voice or as
the feeling found a form. Nothing is pure, after all. The
shell is cool on the shelf. Your shoulders ache from rowing
for an hour on the lake. A dog swam there with his master.
The fireflies are invisible in the hedges. The shelf is cool
under the shell. Nothing must happen behind your back.
The world must be perfect and whole. You must ignore the
tapping, tapping, tapping on the sidewalk in summer.

You must ignore the wingy whirr in the crabapple tree. You must ignore the crack of the stair in the dark. We live in such a narrow house. The door scrapes our heads. The window is our eyes' size. There is something you should know. There is something else. The mainspring of love wears out, loses its force. It falls behind time, further and further. It never catches up again. Or there is something else. Or there are two pleasures only. Or they are the same pleasure with different faces. Or remembering a face is like remembering the clock. Was it brass or bronze? Were the numerals Arabic or Roman? Were those angels on top or birds? Or the average person learns and remembers ten thousand faces in his lifetime. It is not true that if you do not understand now, someday you will understand. I will tell you what is true. The eglantine is true. Only the eglantine.

Nominated for the National Book Award and nominated three times for the Pulitzer Prize, J. R. SOLONCHE is the author of over thirty books of poetry and coauthor of another. He lives in the Hudson Valley.